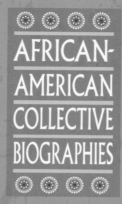

AFRICAN-
AMERICAN
COLLECTIVE
BIOGRAPHIES

Amazing African-American Actors

Jeff C. Young

Enslow Publishers, Inc.
40 Industrial Road
Box 398
Berkeley Heights, NJ 07922
USA

http://www.enslow.com

To the victims of the Orangeburg Massacre:
Samuel Hammond, Delano Middleton and Henry Smith.

Library of Congress Cataloging-in-Publication Data
Young, Jeff.
  Amazing African-American actors / Jeff Young.
    p. cm. — (African-American collective biographies)
  Summary: "Read about ten important African-American actors including: Paul Robeson,
Ossie Davis, Dorothy Dandridge, Ruby Dee, Sidney Poitier, Morgan Freeman, Denzel Wash-
ington, Whoopi Goldberg, Jamie Foxx, and Halle Berry"—Provided by publisher.
  Includes bibliographical references and index.
  ISBN 978-1-59845-135-1 (alk. paper)
  1. African-American actors—Biography—Juvenile literature. 2. African-American motion
picture actors and actresses Juvenile literature.—Biography I. Title.
  PN2286.Y65 2010
  791.4302'8092396073—dc23
  [B]   2011019951

Future editions
Paperback ISBN 978-1-4644-0034-6
ePUB ISBN 978-1-4645-0941-4
PDF ISBN 978-1-4646-0941-1

Printed in the United States of America
032012 Lake Book Manufacturing, Inc., Melrose Park, IL

10 9 8 7 6 5 4 3 2 1

To Our Readers: We have done our best to make sure all Internet Addresses in this book
were active and appropriate when we went to press. However, the author and the publisher
have no control over and assume no liability for the material available on those Internet
sites or on other Web sites they may link to. Any comments or suggestions can be sent by
e-mail to comments@enslow.com or to the address on the back cover.

Enslow Publishers, Inc., is committed to printing our books on recycled paper. The
paper in every book contains 10% to 30% post-consumer waste (PCW). The cover board
on the outside of each book contains 100% PCW. Our goal is to do our part to help young
people and the environment too!

Photo Credits: AP Images, pp. 38, 51; AP Images: Bob Galbraith, p. 79, Doug Mills, pp. 64,
92, Mark J. Terrill, p. 56, Reed Saxon, p. 84; Columbia Pictures/courtesy Everett Collection,
p. 20; CSU Archives/courtesy Everett Collection, pp. 15, 23; Everett Collection, pp. 6, 7,
8, 30, 34, 46; © HBO/courtesy Everett Collection, p. 96; Library of Congress, p. 10; Mary
Evans/Ronald Grant/Everett Collection, p. 68; Mary Evans/© 2004 Warner Bros. Entertainment Inc. All Rights Reserved/Ronald Grant/courtesy Everett Collection, p. 59; © Universal
Pictures/courtesy Everett Collection, p. 42; © Warner Brothers/courtesy Everett Collection,
pp. 79, 87.

Cover Illustration: AP Images/Doug Mills

Contents

Introduction

In the early days of filmmaking, roles for African-American actors were very hard to come by. Even when the script called for an African American, the part would be played by a white actor. According to the book *Black Firsts*, the first appearance of blacks in films was in a 1902 French film entitled *Off to Bloomingdale Asylum*. It's believed that the black characters in that film were played by white actors.

In D. W. Griffith's controversial-but-epic 1915 film *The Birth of a Nation*, the roles of sinister African-American characters were played by white actors wearing blackface makeup. When an African-American actor did get a role at that time, it was usually a demeaning one. In those days, the most common roles for African-American actors were servant, villain, or some sort of buffoon. That sort of typecasting and racial stereotyping would continue for many years.

But thanks to the efforts of some pioneering African-American and white filmmakers, there were a few movies produced in the early twentieth century that portrayed African Americans in a more favorable light.

Based in Jacksonville, Florida, Richard E. Norman was a white film producer who made a handful of films in the 1920s, including some that portrayed African Americans as cowboys, airplane pilots, and boat captains. The men he cast in those roles were depicted as brave and resourceful.

"Norman was one of the few white filmmakers who did make these race films, and he did a good job of making movies that were of quality and had positive images of African-Americans in a period when the movie industry as a whole really was devoted to disseminating a very negative image of blacks," said University of North Florida history professor Carolyn Williams.[1]

Norman is credited with producing six feature films between 1920 and 1928. In addition to providing positive role models for African Americans, Norman's films gave stage-trained African-American actors a chance to act on film. But when silent movies were replaced by the "talkies," Norman's small studio was unable to survive the change. (An effort is currently under way to create a Jacksonville tourist attraction out of the five still-standing buildings of Norman Studios.)

Oscar Micheaux is regarded as the most prolific and successful of the early African-American filmmakers. After raising $15,000 from small investors, Micheaux produced his first film, *The Homesteader*, in 1919. He went on to make some forty-odd movies between 1919 and 1948. His 1924 film *Body and Soul* featured the screen debut of noted African-American actor Paul Robeson.

Micheaux's films didn't shy away from controversial topics and issues. They dealt with interracial marriages, racial prejudice, African Americans passing themselves off as white, hypocritical preachers, and the harassment of African Americans by the Ku Klux Klan. Sometimes his films were censored, and he was forced to cut out certain scenes.

By the 1930s, Micheaux's films had fallen out of favor with most African-American filmgoers. The African-American press attacked him for his apparent preference for light-skinned black actors, whom he cast as middle-class professionals at a time when most African Americans lived in poverty.

Hollywood films in the 1930s were subject to a strict code of self-censorship. Because of that, African Americans were largely restricted to playing roles as servants to white employers. In 1939, Hattie McDaniel became the first African American to win an Academy Award. She won the award for playing a plantation slave in the Civil War drama *Gone With the Wind*.

Oscar Micheaux, one of the earliest African-American filmmakers, made more than forty films in less than three decades.

6

In the 1940s and 1950s the film industry showed a greater willingness to explore racial issues and to offer better and more varied parts to African-American actors. *Pinky* (1949) examined the problems of a light-skinned African-American woman passing herself off as white. *Intruder in the Dust* (1949) portrayed an elderly white woman teaming up with a young white boy to prevent an African American from being lynched for a crime that he didn't commit. *No Way Out* (1950) showed

Introduction

how an African-American family and neighborhood came together to defend themselves from the threat of racism.

The 1960s saw the emergence of Sidney Poitier as an Academy Award–winning international film star. On television shows *The Mod Squad*, *I Spy*, *Julia*, and *East Side/West Side*, African Americans took on roles as regular cast members.

During the last three decades of the twentieth century the film industry offered more opportunities for

Actress Hattie McDaniel (right, with Vivien Leigh) won an Academy Award for Best Supporting Actress in *Gone With the Wind*.

I Spy

Bill Cosby (left) and Robert Culp starred in *I Spy*, an NBC television drama that aired from 1965 to 1968.

African Americans not just as actors, but as camera operators, makeup artists, carpenters, and electricians.

As roles for African-American actors have become more common, the number of African-American actors winning major acting awards has greatly increased. In the past quarter century, African-American actors Halle Berry, Jamie Foxx, Denzel Washington, Morgan Freeman, Jennifer Hudson, Cuba Gooding Jr., Whoopi Goldberg, and Forest Whitaker have all won Academy Awards. Many other African-American actors have won or been nominated for such major awards as the Golden Globes and the Emmys.

Today actors of their stature can command multimillion-dollar salaries for starring in big-budget productions. They've also made it easier for African-American directors, producers, and screenwriters to gain access to studio executives for pitching their projects and ideas.

There is no question that significant progress has been made, but it's not something that can be taken for granted. As African-American author and film historian Donald Bogle noted, "The old walls and barriers had been—at least partially— knocked down."[2]

Whether they stay down permanently remains to be seen.

Paul Robeson
in 1942

Paul Robeson

To call Paul Robeson an actor ignores his many other achievements during an eventful and controversial life. He was also a scholar of languages, an attorney, a gifted athlete, a civil rights activist, and a renowned singer and recording artist. Robeson was an outspoken, opinionated man who didn't waver from his convictions. For boldly expressing his thoughts and beliefs, he lost both his freedom to travel and his once-promising career as an entertainer.

Paul was born in Princeton, New Jersey, on April 9, 1898, the youngest of five children. His father, William, was a runaway slave who worked his way through college to become a minister. His mother, Louisa, died when he was only five. William was a strict father who expected his youngest child to be involved in the church, hardworking, a good student, and an obedient son.

Apparently, Paul was all of those things, but he seldom received approval or affection from his father. Robeson would later write: "It was not like him to be demonstrative in his love, nor was he quick to praise."[1]

When he was seventeen, Robeson won a statewide competition for a four-year scholarship to Rutgers University. While at Rutgers, he excelled in both academics and athletics. He was elected to the Phi Beta Kappa honor society and was also selected as the valedictorian of his class. Outside of the classroom, Robeson lettered in four sports—baseball, basketball, football, and track. He became the first Rutgers athlete to be named to Walter Camp's All-American football team.

After earning a B.A. degree from Rutgers in 1919, Robeson studied law at Columbia University in New York City. He worked his way through law school by tutoring and by playing professional football. Robeson played for the Akron Pros in 1920 and the Milwaukee Badgers in the following year.

A football injury led Robeson to meet his future wife. While recovering from surgery at New York Presbyterian Hospital, Robeson was introduced to a lab technician named Eslanda Goode. Robeson became very attracted to her, and they were married in August 1921.

Robeson received his law degree from Columbia in 1923 and began working for a prominent law firm headed by another Rutgers graduate. Robeson was the only African-American attorney in the firm, and he was not warmly received by his coworkers. He left the firm after a secretary refused to take dictation from him. She had told him that she would never take dictation from an African American.

By the time he had left the law firm, Robeson had already begun acting in amateur productions. He joined a theater group known as the Provincetown Players. The leading member of the group was noted playwright Eugene O'Neill, who would later win the Nobel Prize in literature.

Robeson made his Broadway debut in 1922 in the play *Taboo*. The Broadway version ended after only four performances, but the play enjoyed a longer run in London. Appearing in the London production gave Robeson his first chance to travel outside of the United States. The relative lack of racial prejudice by the British toward African Americans made Robeson more sensitive to and disturbed by the racism he encountered in America.

After returning to the United States, Robeson starred in two plays written by O'Neill, *The Emperor Jones* and *All God's Chillun Got Wings*. Both plays debuted in 1924, and they established Robeson's acting career. The *New York Times* called Robeson's performance in *The Emperor Jones* "singularly fine."[2] Theater critic George Jean Nathan praised Robeson's work in *All God's Chillun Got Wings*, calling him "a born actor."[3]

Robeson also made his movie debut in 1924, in the silent film *Body and Soul*. The film was produced by pioneering African-American filmmaker Oscar Micheaux. Robeson played dual roles, as a fast-talking, corrupt preacher and his sincere, good-hearted brother.

Although it would be six years before he landed another film role, Robeson worked steadily as a stage actor and concert singer. In 1925, the play *The Emperor Jones* made its London debut. A year later, Robeson starred in the play *Black Boy*, which was loosely based on the life of Jack Johnson, the first African-American heavyweight boxing champion. Robeson won further critical acclaim for his work as the title character in Shakespeare's *Othello* and in the musical *Show Boat*.

When he wasn't acting, Robeson was attracting an international following for his work as a singer and recording artist. A 1941 biographical sketch stated that after his 1925 debut as a concert singer, "Robeson's rich,

communicative baritone voice…made itself heard and felt all over the world. He became even more popular as a singer of Negro spirituals than as an actor, and as well known in London and Moscow as in New York."[4]

During the 1930s, Robeson spent most of his time acting onstage and giving concerts outside of the United States. The films *The Emperor Jones* (1933) and *Show Boat* (1936) allowed him to repeat two of his most successful stage roles. For the latter film, the mainstream press praised Robeson's acting, but the black press criticized him harshly for playing a role that was considered demeaning and offensive to African Americans.

In 1934, Robeson made the first of several trips to the Soviet Union. His musical recordings were quite popular there, and he was warmly received. What may have made the deepest impression on him was the absence of racial bias and prejudice among his Russian hosts. In the United States, Robeson had been denied service in hotels and restaurants because of his race. When he was in Moscow, he wrote: "Here, for the first time in my life, I walk in full human dignity."[5]

Robeson began making public statements criticizing the United States for its racism and praising the Soviet Union for its perceived racial tolerance. But while he was extolling the Soviet Union, he overlooked or didn't mention the purges of political opponents by its brutal dictator, Josef Stalin. Stalin was responsible for the deaths of millions of Russians who dared to oppose his oppressive rule.

After appearing in the film version of *Show Boat*, Robeson became convinced that the American film industry would never provide him with the types of roles he wanted to play.

He limited his film appearances to British productions. Between 1936 and 1940, he appeared in five British films.

Song of Freedom (1936) was the first of his British films. Robeson played a British dockworker who becomes an internationally famous concert singer. Robeson was pleased to star in a film that portrayed blacks favorably,

Paul Robeson (left), with his wife, Eslanda, and their son, Paul Robeson, Jr.

but the film attracted little attention and was never distributed to American movie theaters.

None of Robeson's other British films are particularly notable. *Jericho* (1937) is generally considered to be the best of the bunch. Robeson plays Jericho Jackson, a World War II draftee who deserts the army to avoid an unjust court-martial. Jackson wanders across North Africa before marrying the daughter of a tribal chieftain. Jackson becomes the leader of the tribe while eluding and outwitting the white authorities who try to capture him.

After returning to America in 1939, Robeson was involved in only two more films. *Native Land* (1942) was a documentary about labor union organizing. Robeson provided the narration. *Tales of Manhattan* (1942) was his final film. Robeson was reportedly outraged by how he and two other African-American actors, Eddie Anderson and Ethel Waters, were portrayed. They played sharecroppers who were depicted as naïve and almost childlike. A review in the New York newspaper *Amsterdam Star News* called Robeson's character "simple-minded" and "docile."[6]

After the premiere of *Tales of Manhattan*, Robeson called a press conference to announce that he would never appear in another Hollywood movie. But he continued to work as a stage actor. His 1943 Broadway portrayal of Othello was one of the best-reviewed and most satisfying roles of his career. A review in the *New York Times* noted that after the play's opening night performance, the audience demanded at least ten curtain calls. The review praised Robeson's performance by noting: "His final speech about being a man 'who loved not wisely but too well' is magnificent. He passes easily along the various stages of Othello's growing jealousy. He can be alike a commanding figure, accustomed to lead, a lover willing to be led and the insane victim of his own ill judgment."[7]

Because of his outspoken admiration of the Soviet Union and his statements and speeches criticizing racial segregation and inequality in the United States, Robeson's career went into a rapid decline after the end of World War II. In 1950, the U.S. State Department revoked his passport because he refused to say if he had ever been a member of the Communist party. After years of legal battles, Robeson got it back in 1958. His last acting performance was repeating the role of Othello at Stratford-on-Avon, England, in 1959.

After regaining his passport, Robeson lived in London and continued to visit the Soviet Union. Still, he never gave up his American citizenship and he returned to live in the United States in 1963. In his final years, Robeson was plagued by depression, failing health, and an addiction to prescription drugs. He died of a stroke in Philadelphia on January 23, 1976.

Paul Robeson Timeline

1898—Born in Princeton, New Jersey on April 9.

1904—His mother Louisa dies.

1917–1918—Twice chosen to Walter Camp's All-American football team while attending Rutgers University.

1919—Graduates from Rutgers University.

1920–1921—Plays pro football while attending law school at Columbia University.

1921—Marries Eslanda Goode.

1923—Graduates from Columbia University Law School.

1924—Makes movie debut in the silent film *Body and Soul*. Appears in Eugene O'Neill plays *The Emperor Jones* and *All God's Chillun Got Wings*.

1925—Launches his career as a singer and recording artist.

1928—Moves to London and acts and sings in the musical *Show Boat*.

1930—Plays title role in Shakespeare's *Othello*.

1934—Visits Soviet Union for the first time.

1942—Makes final film appearance in *Tales of Manhattan*.

Timeline

1943—Stars in a Broadway production of *Othello*.

1950—Has passport revoked by the U.S. State Department.

1958—Has passport reissued after a lengthy legal battle.

1959—Gives final performance as Othello.

1963—Returns to the United States to live.

1965—Wife Eslanda dies.

1976—Dies in Philadelphia, Pennsylvania, on January 23.

Ossie Davis in *Get On the Bus* in 1996

Ossie Davis

Acting brought Ossie Davis and Ruby Dee together, and they stayed together for over half a century. During that time, they distinguished themselves both as award-winning actors and as activists in the civil rights movement. They have also served as role models and mentors for generations of African-American actors.

Ossie Davis was born on December 18, 1917, in Cogdell, Georgia. He was the oldest of four children. His given name was Raiford Chatman Davis, but when a courthouse clerk asked Ossie's mother for his name, she said "R.C." The clerk then recorded his name as Ossie.

"Mama would not have argued with him," Davis recalled. "The man was white. Mama and I were black and down in deepest Georgia. So the matter of identification was settled. Ossie it was."[1]

Ossie's father, Kince Charles Davis, was a railroad construction worker. His mother, Laura Cooper, was a homemaker. After graduating from high school in 1934, Ossie had scholarship offers from Savannah State College in Georgia and the Tuskegee Institute in Alabama.

Ossie had both the desire and discipline to pursue a college degree, but even with scholarships, he didn't have enough money to pay for it. He spent a year working in a pharmacy before enrolling at Howard University in Washington, D.C. At Howard, Ossie took classes taught by drama critic Alain Locke. Ossie credits Locke with "giving me my life."[2] Locke encouraged Ossie to pursue his goal of becoming a playwright. He also advised Ossie to go to New York City and learn about the theater by working with Off-Broadway acting groups.

Davis followed Locke's advice after leaving Howard in 1939. He settled in New York City and joined the Rose McClendon Players, a theatrical troupe based in Harlem. He appeared in four plays between 1939 and 1941 while learning the basics of acting, stagecraft, and playwriting.

Davis's budding theatrical career was interrupted when he was drafted into the U.S. Army in 1942. After being discharged in 1945, he returned to New York. His first role after leaving the army was the title role in Robert Ardey's Broadway play *Jeb* (1946). Davis played a returning war hero amputee who faces down the Ku Klux Klan before marrying his girlfriend. His future wife, Ruby Dee, costarred as his girlfriend, Libby.

Davis's Broadway debut was well regarded. A review in the *New York Times* called his acting "straightforward and often touching."[3] Unfortunately, reviews for the play itself were less favorable. *Jeb* closed after only nine performances.

22

Davis and Dee continued to see each other after the play's run ended. They were married in 1948 while rehearsing for the Broadway play *Smile of the World*.

Davis appeared in fifteen plays between 1948 and 1957. His role in the Broadway play *Jamaica* earned him a Tony Award nomination. During that time, he also began

Ossie Davis and Ruby Dee in 1946

working as a film actor. His first movie appearance came in 1950 in *No Way Out*. Davis and Dee played supporting roles to the star Sidney Poitier. Poitier played a young doctor who is falsely accused of killing a white patient.

In 1951, Davis made a brief screen appearance in *Fourteen Hours* as a cab driver, but twelve years passed before he landed another movie part. At that time, the movie industry engaged in a practice known as blacklisting. Because of their political beliefs, many actors, screenwriters, producers, and directors were prevented from working in movies, television, and radio.

For a time, Davis had attended meetings of the Young Communist League in Harlem. He never became a Communist, but that didn't keep him and Dee from being blacklisted. They eked out a living by giving presentations in black churches, community centers, and colleges, where they read from the works of notable playwrights, novelists, and poets.

"These appearances taught us how to convert any space into a theater and thus to make our own job opportunities," Davis recalled. "Two notebooks, two music stands or podiums, and our passion for great literature are all that was required to create a kind of people's theater."[4]

After the blacklist ended, Davis was able to return to Broadway productions. One of his more notable roles was playing Cicero in the 1957 musical comedy *Jamaica*, which enjoyed a 555-performance run. Davis's greatest Broadway triumph was the production of his play *Purlie Victorious* in 1961.

Along with writing the play, Davis headlined the cast by playing the title role of Purlie Victorious Judson. Dee costarred as Purlie's avid follower, Lutibelle, and they both received glowing reviews for their performances.

Davis deftly used humor to poke fun at Southern racial attitudes while making the audience aware of the racism that African Americans constantly endured. He explained why he wrote it by saying: "The purpose of Purlie is to point a mocking finger at racial segregation and laugh it out of existence."[5]

As one reviewer noted: "While 'Purlie Victorious' keeps you chuckling and guffawing, it unrelentingly forces you to feel how it is to inhabit a dark skin in a hostile, or at best, grudgingly benevolent world."[6]

Along with his success as a stage actor and playwright, Davis also compiled an impressive body of work as a television and movie actor. He received three Emmy Award nominations. One of them was for playing Dr. Martin Luther King's father in the acclaimed miniseries *King* (1978). Davis's performance was influenced by his relationship with Dr. King. He had been a close friend and strong supporter and had delivered an eloquent eulogy at Dr. King's funeral in 1968.

Davis also made frequent guest appearances on various television shows including *N.Y.P.D.*, *Evening Shade*, and *Bonanza*. He and Dee had their own show on PBS, *With Ossie and Ruby* (1981). His last television role was on the Showtime series *The L Word*. Ironically, the character he played died on the show shortly before his death in 2005. The death episode was broadcast shortly after Davis's death with a dedication to him.

Between 1963 and 2005, Davis appeared in more than forty films. Late in his acting career, he had parts in several of director Spike Lee's films, including *Jungle Fever*, *Do The Right Thing*, and *Get on the Bus*. Davis also directed five films. The most significant was *Cotton Comes to Harlem* (1970), based on a novel by African-American author Chester Himes.

Cotton Comes to Harlem is regarded as a landmark film because it was filmed in Harlem, and because it showed Hollywood film executives that there was a considerable market for films with African-American casts. In his joint autobiography with Dee, Davis called *Cotton Comes to Harlem* "the best thing that I've ever done as a director."[7]

In recognition of his work as an actor, playwright, writer, and civil rights activist, Davis was awarded the Kennedy Center Lifetime Achievement Award in 2004. Davis died in Miami, Florida, on February 4, 2005, but received further honors after his death. At the 2007 Grammy Awards, Davis and Dee won a Grammy for Best Spoken Word Album for their recording of their joint autobiography *In This Life Together*. In a tie vote, they shared the award with former president Jimmy Carter.

Ossie Davis Timeline

1917—Born Raiford Chatman Davis in Cogdell, Georgia, on December 18.

1934—Graduates from Center High School in Waycross, Georgia.

1935–1939—Attends Howard University in Washington, D.C.

1939—Makes acting debut in the play *Joy Exceeding Glory*.

1942–1945—Serves in the U.S. Army in World War II.

1946—Makes Broadway debut playing title role in the play *Jeb*.

1948—Marries Ruby Dee.

1950—Makes movie debut in *No Way Out*.

1957—Receives Tony Award nomination for playing Cicero in the musical *Jamaica*.

1961—Writes and stars in the Broadway play *Purlie Victorious*.

1969—Nominated for an Emmy Award for his role in *Teacher, Teacher*.

1970—Directs the movie *Cotton Comes to Harlem*.

1978—Gets second Emmy Award nomination for playing Dr. Martin Luther King's father in the miniseries *King*.

1989—Receives NAACP Image Award for his role in Spike Lee's film *Do the Right Thing*.

1994—Inducted into the Theater Hall of Fame.

1997—Nominated for an Emmy Award for *Miss Evers' Boys*.

2001—Wins a Daytime Emmy for children's special *Finding Buck McHenry*.

2005—Dies in Miami, Florida, on February 4.

2007—Posthumously wins Grammy Award with wife Ruby Dee for recording of their joint autobiography *In This Life Together*.

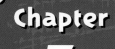

Dorothy Dandridge

If she had been born a couple of decades later, Dorothy Dandridge could have become a major movie star with an international following. She had the talent, the looks, and the will to succeed. As it turned out, she still enjoyed critical acclaim and an Academy Award nomination before broken marriages, bankruptcy, and finally drug dependency ended her career and her short life.

Dorothy Dandridge was born in Cleveland, Ohio, on November 9, 1922. Her father, Cyril, was a Baptist minister and her mother, Ruby, was a radio and movie comedian. Dorothy's parents separated about the time she was born. Ruby pushed Dorothy and her older sister, Vivian, to pursue show business careers. As a child Dorothy sang, danced, and did comedy skits while appearing with her mother and sister.

In 1934, Ruby moved her family to Los Angeles to further her daughters' show business careers. She organized her two daughters and Etta Jones into a singing group called the Dandridge Sisters. After the trio won an amateur talent contest on a Los Angeles radio

Dorothy Dandridge
around 1950

station, they were invited to perform at New York's famous Cotton Club.

From 1920 to 1940, the Cotton Club showcased the most popular and best-known African-American entertainers. Although it was located in Harlem, the club didn't open its doors to African-American customers until 1928. Bandleaders Duke Ellington, Louis Armstrong, and Cab Calloway along with dancers Bill "Bojangles" Robinson and the Nicholas Brothers were some of the club's headline acts.

In 1935 the Dandridge Sisters shot what would become their movie debut, an unbilled appearance in *The Big Broadcast of 1936*. Between 1937 and 1940, they appeared in four more movies. The Dandridge sisters also toured with Duke Ellington and Cab Calloway. They were on an international tour when the United States entered World War II in 1941. That abruptly interrupted their tour and led to the group's breakup.

Dorothy Dandridge found work appearing in a few musical film shorts as a solo singer. In 1942, she married her first husband, Harold Nicholas, a professional dancer. They settled in Los Angeles and pursued movie careers. She found work playing minor roles in films such as *Drums of the Congo*, *The Hit Parade of 1943*, and *Atlantic City*.

Dandridge divorced Nicholas in 1951. During their marriage, he had committed numerous infidelities. He abandoned his family after the birth of their severely mentally retarded daughter Harolyn in 1943.

With a child to support and a lack of acting jobs to sustain her, Dandridge began pursuing a career as a nightclub singer. She appeared in prestigious clubs in Los Angeles; New York; Rio de Janeiro, Brazil; and Paris, France. She could have continued with that career, but

31

her plans changed when she got her first big break as a movie actress.

In 1954, famed movie producer-director Otto Preminger cast her in the title role of *Carmen Jones*. The lavish musical featured an all African-American cast that included Harry Belafonte, Pearl Bailey, and Diahann Carroll. The film was a critical success, and it won a Golden Globe Award for Best Musical Motion Picture. Dandridge received a Best Actress Oscar nomination for her memorable portrayal of Carmen.

Along with the Best Actress nomination, Dandridge's performance as Carmen earned her a host of rave reviews. *Newsweek* called her "one of the outstanding dramatic actresses of the screen."[1] *Time* magazine's review said that Dandridge "holds the eye like a match burning steadily in a tornado."[2] The review in *Time* also predicted that the success of *Carmen Jones* would lead to more opportunities for other African-American actors. But that didn't happen.

Grace Kelly won the Best Actress Oscar for her role in *The Country Girl*. Dandridge didn't get an Oscar, but she did get a contract with 20th Century-Fox to do three more movies in three years. Her future seemed bright, but she only made one film for the studio.

Fox had wanted to cast her in their big-budget version of the hit Broadway musical *The King and I*. Dandridge refused to appear in the movie because she would have to play a slave, and because her contract called for her to be billed as star or costar in any movie she made for Fox.

The King and I was a huge box office success. The film was seen by millions, and it earned nine Academy Award nominations. By being assertive, Dandridge got a reputation for being difficult and ungrateful. She wouldn't make another movie until 1957.

Her next film, *Island in the Sun*, was her only movie for Fox. The film is considered groundbreaking today for its depiction of an interracial romance. When Dandridge was embraced by white actor John Justin, she became the first African-American actress to be hugged by a white man in a Hollywood movie.

The film caused a furor in the South. In South Carolina, the state legislature considered a bill that would have fined any movie theater showing it $5,000. A board of censors in Memphis, Tennessee, banned the film. In Greensboro, North Carolina, a wooden cross was set afire to protest the showing of the film at a local drive-in theater.

Dandridge's next film, *The Decks Ran Red* (1958), hinted at the possibilities of an interracial romance. The film showcased Dandridge's striking good looks, but didn't give her a memorable character to play. The film wasn't a critical or commercial success.

Porgy and Bess (1959) was a big-budget production that won an Academy Award for the Best Scoring of a Musical Picture. Dandridge received mostly negative reviews for her portrayal of Bess, a crude and coarse character. Critics said that Dandridge was too delicate and refined to give a credible performance. The criticisms really stung her because she had wanted to play roles that portrayed African-American women as dignified and refined characters.

Shortly after making *Porgy and Bess*, Dandridge remarried. Her second husband, Jack Denison, was a restaurant and nightclub owner. He got Dandridge to invest in his businesses, which later caused her some financial problems. Denison was a bad husband in addition to being a bad businessman. According to Dandridge

A still photo from *Porgy and Bess* (1959). Dorothy Dandridge (right) starred with Sidney Poitier.

biographer Donald Bogle, Denison was physically and verbally abusive. The couple divorced in 1962.

After divorcing Denison, Dandridge was no longer in demand as an actress or nightclub singer. She also discovered that she had been swindled out of her life savings of $500,000. Along with the loss of income, she was being pressured by the Internal Revenue Service for payment of $139,000 in back taxes. She found work appearing on television shows, but wasn't making enough money to pay off her creditors. In her bankruptcy petition, she listed over $127,000 in debts and only $5,000 in assets.

Dorothy Dandridge

The combination of a crumbling career and persistent financial problems made Dandridge increasingly dependent on prescription antidepressant medications. She died on September 8, 1965. Her autopsy revealed that an overdose of Imipramine, an antidepressant drug, was the cause of her death. An investigation ruled that the overdose was a "probable accident"[3] and not a suicide.

In an interview published shortly after her death, Dandridge summed up the difficulties she had faced in finding roles that portrayed African-American women in a favorable light: "I consider myself an actress, and I have always worked to be a confident one. I interpret a role to the best of my ability, and more often than I'd like, the role calls for a creature of abandon whose desires are stronger than their sense of morality."[4]

The African-American entertainment community continued to hold her in high regard. In 1999 Halle Berry starred in a biographical film drama entitled *Introducing Dorothy Dandridge*. In that same year, Dandridge's name was entered on the Hollywood Walk of Fame.

Dorothy Dandridge Timeline

1922—Born in Cleveland, Ohio, on November 9.

1934—Dorothy's mother, Ruby, moves family to Los Angeles so her two daughters can pursue careers in show business.

1936—Makes first film appearance, in *The Big Broadcast of 1936*.

1942—Marries dancer/entertainer Harold Nicholas.

1943—Daughter Harolyn is born.

1951—Divorces Harold Nicholas.

1954—Receives Academy Award Best Actress nomination for her role in *Carmen Jones*. She becomes the first African-American woman to be nominated for the award.

1959—Marries restaurant/nightclub owner Jack Denison.

1962—Divorces Jack Denison.

1963—Declares bankruptcy.

1965—Dies in West Hollywood, California, on September 8.

1999—*Introducing Dorothy Dandridge*, a movie tribute to her life starring Halle Berry, is released.

Ruby Dee

Ruby Dee was a shy and somewhat passive child who saw acting as a way of overcoming her shyness and communicating what she felt but couldn't express.

In an interview, Ruby admitted that during her childhood she was "painfully shy and not at all aggressive,"[1] but then she added, "I had wild feelings churning inside me that I wanted to express."[2]

Ruby Ann Wallace was born in Cleveland, Ohio, on October 27, 1924. Her father, Edward Nathaniel Wallace, was a railroad waiter and porter who was divorced by Gladys Hightower shortly after Ruby's birth. Her father then married Emma Amelia Benson, a schoolteacher who insisted that Ruby and her three siblings study music and literature.

Ruby was an infant when her family moved to Harlem. By the time she was in high school Ruby had decided to become an actress. Her stepmother approved, but only if Ruby became a serious actress. Serious meant being steadily employed in the field and earning a living.

When Ruby entered Hunter College in 1939, she majored in romance languages instead of taking classes

Ossie Davis and Ruby Dee at the premier of their movie *Gone Are the Days* in 1963.

in theater and acting. She still wanted to act, but she needed something that offered greater security and job opportunities.

> I wanted to be an actor but the chances for success did not look promising," Ruby explained. "Most blacks in film or on stage played servants, exotics, criminals or comics. Concentrating on studying theater and related topics just didn't seem practical or important enough.... 'In case you don't make it as an actor, you'll have something to fall back on,' was the general advice.[3]

But even while taking a full load of college classes, Ruby gamely pursued her acting dreams. From 1941 to 1944, she worked as an apprentice for the American Negro Theater. Along with acting, she painted scenery, mopped the floors, and sold tickets. In December 1943 she made her Broadway debut with a small, nonspeaking part in a play titled *South Pacific* (not the Broadway hit musical). She also found occasional jobs acting in radio plays.

After earning a B.A. from Hunter College in 1945, Dee used her knowledge of French and Spanish to work as a translator for an import business. That job only lasted for a brief time. Acting became her focus after appearances in the plays *Jeb* (1946) and *Anna Lucasta* (1946–1947). In both of those plays, she acted with her future husband, Ossie Davis.

During the rehearsals for *Jeb*, Dee first realized that she might have some tender, romantic feelings for Davis. She was watching Davis rehearse a scene where he began to slowly tie his necktie. In her autobiography, she writes: "At that moment, I distinctly remember feeling something like a bolt of lightning, an electrical charge, flash between us. Although I didn't move, I felt a physical jolt."[4]

39

Ruby Dee and Ossie Davis got married in December 1948 during a break in rehearsals for the play *Smile of the World*. They didn't have time to go on a honeymoon. While working as a two-career couple, they still managed to raise two girls and a boy.

Exactly when Dee made her first movie appearance is a matter of dispute. One source claims that she was in the all African-American cast movie *What A Guy* (1939), which would mean that she made her movie debut while she was in high school. A second source claims that her debut was in *The Jackie Robinson Story* (1950). According to her autobiography, *The Fight Never Ends* (1947) was her first film.

There is agreement that her first significant film role was in *Edge of the City* (1957) with Sidney Poitier. Dee played Poitier's supportive wife who loses him after he is murdered during a fight with his bullying boss. One review singled out Dee's role by saying: "Of particular note in the cast is Ruby Dee, who renders a fine supporting performance as Poitier's loyal wife, Lucy. She is especially moving when she breaks down after learning from North of her husband's death."[5]

Another important role in Dee's acting career was one she played both onstage and on film: Ruth Younger in *A Raisin in the Sun*. Once again she was cast as Sidney Poitier's wife. The plot revolves around the hopes of the Younger family. Three generations of the family are living in a cramped three-room Chicago apartment. They ultimately realize their collective dream of leaving the apartment and owning their own home.

Dee's stage performance as Ruth earned her much critical acclaim. But her film portrayal was even more highly praised. In a review in the *New Yorker*, film critic Edith Oliver wrote that Dee's film performance was "even

more impressive than it was on stage," and added, "Is there a better young actress in America, or one who can make everything she does seem so effortless?"[6]

In 1965, Dee fulfilled a lifelong dream to act in plays by William Shakespeare. By doing so, she became the first African-American actress to appear in major roles at the prestigious American Shakespeare Festival. Dee played Kate in *The Taming of the Shrew* and Cordelia in *King Lear.* She also appeared in productions of other classical plays including *The Birds* by the Greek playwright Aristophanses, and Anton Chekov's *The Cherry Orchard.*

Along with her stage and screen work, Dee has a long list of credits in television and radio. In 1991, she won an Emmy Award for her performance in the Hallmark Hall of Fame Production of *Decoration Day.* Dee has also been nominated for an Emmy five other times and for a Daytime Emmy three times.

Following Ossie Davis's death in 2005, Dee has continued to act. In 2007, she received her first Academy Award nomination, for playing Denzel Washington's mother in *American Gangster.* At eighty-three years old, she became the second-oldest actress to receive an Academy Award nomination.

Dee's key scene in *American Gangster* comes when she realizes that her drug kingpin son has become a truly evil person. Prior to that, she had turned a blind eye to his gangster lifestyle. She confronts him over his criminal behavior and gives him a hard slap across the face.

41

"It was her moment of recognition that something had gone wrong in her son's life even though she loved him," Dee told Susan King of the *Los Angeles Times.* "After I saw the whole film, the slap was very well justified; it made up for her blindness."[7]

Ruby Dee and Denzel Washington in a scene from the 2007 film *American Gangster*

42

Along with lengthy and distinguished acting careers, Dee and Davis have devoted themselves to promoting racial equality. They have been active members of the National Association for the Advancement of Colored People (NAACP), Congress of Racial Equality (CORE), the Student Nonviolent Coordinating Committee (SNCC) and the Southern Christian Leadership Conference (SCLC). She has also established the Ruby Dee Scholarship in

Dramatic Art to help young and talented African-American women to enter the acting profession.

Well into her eighties, Dee has no desire to quit working. Her film *The Middle of Nowhere* was released in 2010.

> *"I didn't grow up with professionals that retired,"* Dee said. *"I thought that retiring was when you are tired and go to bed. I am writing a great deal. I am writing plays. I have also conducted workshops and I have ideas yet to bring to fruition. My whole life is not defined by what Hollywood does."*[8]

Ruby Dee Timeline

1924—Born Ruby Ann Wallace in Cleveland, Ohio, on October 27.

1939—Graduates from Hunter College High School in New York City.

1940—Makes acting debut in the play *On Striver's Row*.

1941–1944—Works as an apprentice with the American Negro Theater.

1943—Makes Broadway debut in the play *South Pacific*.

1945—Graduates with a B.A. from Hunter College.

1946—Appears in Broadway play *Jeb* with Ossie Davis.

1948—Marries Ossie Davis.

1957—Wins critical acclaim for her role as Sidney Poitier's wife in the film *Edge of the City*.

1959—Role of Ruth Younger in the Broadway play *A Raisin in the Sun* brings favorable reviews and critical acclaim.

1961—Recreates role of Ruth Younger in film version of *A Raisin in the Sun*. Appears with husband Ossie Davis in the Broadway production of his play *Purlie Victorious*.

1964—Receives first Emmy Award nomination.

Timeline

1965—Becomes the first African-American actress to play major roles in the American Shakespeare Festival.

1970—Wins Obie Award and Drama Desk Award for role in the play *Boesman and Lena*.

1988—Inducted into the Theater Hall of Fame.

1991—Wins Emmy Award for role in Hallmark Hall of Fame production of *Decoration Day*.

2001—Receives Lifetime Achievement Award from the Screen Actors Guild.

2007—Wins Grammy Award with husband Ossie Davis for recording of their joint autobiography.

2007—Receives Academy Award Nomination for Best Supporting Actress in *American Gangster*.

2008—Role in *American Gangster* wins her the Screen Actors Guild Award for Outstanding Performance by a Female Actor in a Supporting Role.

2010—Narrates *Broadway: Beyond the Golden Age*.

2010—Receives Image Award for Outstanding Actress in a Television Movie, Mini-Series or Dramatic Special for *America*.

Sidney Poitier in *A Patch of Blue*

Chapter 5

Sidney Poitier

There have been other famous African–American actors and film stars before and after Sidney Poitier, but few, if any, have had such a lasting impact in changing racial attitudes in the film and entertainment business. One biographical profile of him noted:

> In his long and distinguished career, Sidney Poitier has broken down every barrier placed in his path. Until his arrival in Hollywood, most black actors had been relegated to demeaning roles that favored stereotype over substance; with his fierce good looks and quiet, measured eloquence, Poitier swiftly rose above those conventions to become the most prominent black American actor of his and possibly any generation.[1]

Poitier was born in Miami Beach, Florida, on February 20, 1927. When he was born, his parents, Reginald and Evelyn Poitier, were visiting Miami from their home in the Bahamas.

Sidney weighed only three pounds at birth, and his parents were deeply concerned that he would not live long. In his autobiography, Poitier writes that his mother visited a local soothsayer who told her: "Don't worry about your son…He will survive and he will not be a sickly child. He will...travel to most of the corners of the earth. He will walk with kings. He will be rich and famous. Your name will be carried all over the world."[2]

Sidney grew up in humble surroundings on Cat Island, a three-mile-wide strip of land in the Bahamas. The house he shared with his six brothers and sisters lacked plumbing and electricity. He wore clothes that were woven from discarded flour sacks. Sidney would escape from his surroundings by taking solitary walks on the beach and by imagining what lay beyond the tiny island.

When Sidney was ten, his family moved to Nassau, the capital city of the Bahamas. His new home was a completely different world from what he had known. It was a bustling tourist town full of bars, nightclubs, hotels, movie theaters, and dance halls.

In this faster-paced environment, Sidney eventually landed in trouble with the law. During his teens, he was briefly jailed for stealing corn. After Sidney was released, his father sent him to Miami to live with an older brother.

In Miami, Sidney encountered racial prejudice and police harassment. While he was walking home one evening, the police picked him up and held a pistol to his forehead. They let him go after joking about shooting him in the eye. That incident convinced Sidney to leave Miami for New York City.

Sidney found work as a dishwasher, but he couldn't find or afford a place to live. After being arrested for vagrancy, he lied about his age and enlisted in the army. He was only sixteen. The army gave him food and a place to sleep, but he deeply disliked the military and wished to get out. He got his wish when he was discharged for throwing a chair at an officer.

He returned to New York with no job and no immediate prospects of finding one. One day, he saw a help-wanted newspaper ad that said ACTORS WANTED. That put Sidney on the path that would change his life.

Sidney thought that acting couldn't be any harder than washing dishes. But he quickly found out how wrong he was. His first audition was a disaster. He stumbled through his lines in his thick Bahamian accent. The director grabbed the script from Sidney and physically removed him from the theater. As a parting shot, he told Sidney to get a job he could handle—like being a dishwasher.

A lesser person would have been crushed by such a stinging and cruel rejection. For Sidney, it merely increased his resolve to succeed: "There's something inside me—pride, ego, sense of self—that hates to fail at anything. I could never accept such a verdict of failure."[3]

Poitier bought a radio and began repeating and mimicking the voices he heard until he got rid of his accent. Six months after his initial rejection, he returned to the theater and got hired as a member of their acting company. To help ensure his employment, Poitier also agreed to work as the theater's janitor.

After acting in such plays as *Lysistrata*, *Anna Lucasta*, and *On Striver's Row*, Poitier landed his first part in a Hollywood movie. In *No Way Out* (1950), he played Luther Brooks, a doctor who is blamed for the death of a patient he operated on. The patient's death made him the target of a racist criminal.

49

No Way Out was a commercial success, and Poitier's sympathetic performance led to other movie roles. In *Cry the Beloved Country* (1952), he played a South African priest helping another priest to locate his wayward son.

The Blackboard Jungle (1955) had Poitier playing a tough, defiant high school student who was unwilling to learn.

The movie role that made Poitier an in-demand actor also earned him his first Academy Award nomination—the escaped prison inmate Noah Cullen in *The Defiant Ones* (1958). When Noah makes his escape from the chain-gang road crew, he's shackled to a white prisoner named Joker Jackson (Tony Curtis) by a three-foot chain. The two escapees hate each other, but they're forced to try to get along while trying to elude a pursuing posse.

The Defiant Ones received eight Academy Award nominations. Poitier became the first African-American actor to be nominated for Best Actor. Tony Curtis also received a Best Actor nomination. A review in the *New York Times* praised both actors' performances: "Between the two principal performers there isn't much room for a choice. Mr. Poitier stands out as the Negro convict and Mr. Curtis is surprisingly good. Both men are intensely dynamic. Mr. Poitier shows a deep and powerful strain of underlying compassion."[4]

Once *The Defiant Ones* established Poitier's reputation as a talented actor and box-office draw, other good movie roles followed. Poitier's performances in *All the Young Men* (1960) and *A Raisin in the Sun* (1961) were both well received. In *All the Young Men*, Poitier starred as a Korean War soldier who assumes command of a platoon and forces the men to confront and examine their racial attitudes.

In *A Raisin in the Sun*, he played Walter Lee Younger, a role he had also played onstage. Walter Lee is in conflict with his mother over how the proceeds from his father's life insurance policy should be spent. When she refuses to allow him to invest the funds in a liquor store, he accuses her of trying to dictate her children's lives. But

Sidney Poitier with his Oscar statuette at the 36th Annual Academy Awards in 1964. He won Best Actor for his role in *Lillies of the Field*.

after she gives most of the money to Walter Lee, he loses it in an investment scheme.

Theater critic Brooks Atkinson singled out Poitier's stage portrayal of Walter Lee by writing: "Mr. Poitier is a remarkable actor with enormous power that is always under control....He is as eloquent when he has nothing to say as when he has a pungent line to speak."[5]

Poitier's portrayal of Homer Smith in *Lilies of the Field* (1963) earned him both Academy Award and Golden Globe awards for Best Actor. It also made him the first African American to win the coveted Academy Award for Best Actor.

Lilies of the Field was a low-budget, black-and-white film that was shot in only thirteen days. Still, it won five Academy Award nominations. Homer is a construction worker who helps a group of German nuns by building them a chapel in the Arizona desert. He works without pay and threatens to leave several times before the chapel is finally finished.

A review by Janet St. Clair called Poitier's award-winning performance "humorous and believable"[6] and added that Homer "has no special talents or achievements; he is simply a nice man who has a big heart."[7]

Poitier's status as a major film star became even more firmly established in 1967 when he starred in three of the year's best-received and most commercially successful films, *To Sir With Love*, *In the Heat of the Night*, and *Guess Who's Coming to Dinner*. In the first film, he played an engineer turned teacher in a tough London school.

In the Heat of the Night had Poitier playing Virgil Tibbs, a Philadelphia police detective who becomes involved in an effort to solve a murder in Mississippi. The film won five Academy Awards and became the basis for two sequels and a television series.

In *Guess Who's Coming to Dinner* Poitier costarred with Hollywood legends Spencer Tracy and Katherine Hepburn. They played the parents of Poitier's white fiancée. The movie earned two Academy Awards. It was considered groundbreaking for its time because it explored themes of interracial romance and marriage.

During the 1970s and 1980s, Poitier began directing some of the films he appeared in.

The western *Buck and the Preacher* (1972) was the first of these. The comedies *Uptown Saturday Night* (1974) and *Let's Do It Again* (1975) were commercial successes that met with generally favorable reviews. *Stir Crazy* (1980), with Richard Pryor and Gene Wilder, was the best reviewed and is largely regarded as the funniest of his comedy films.

During the 1990s, Poitier's television work won him further honors. He won an Emmy nomination for his portrayal of lawyer and Supreme Court justice Thurgood Marshall in *Separate but Equal* (1991). His portrayal of South African president and former political prisoner Nelson Mandela in the television film *Mandela and DeKlerk* won him a second Emmy nomination in 1997. That same year he was knighted by England's Queen Elizabeth II.

Poitier's large and distinguished body of work as an actor has also earned him Lifetime Achievement awards from both the American Film Institute (1992) and the Screen Actors Guild (1999). In 2001, he was given an Academy Honorary Award. While presenting the award, Academy president Frank Pierson summed up Poitier's many accomplishments by saying, "When the academy honors Sidney Poitier, it honors itself even more."[8]

Sidney Poitier Timeline

1927—Born in Miami Beach, Florida, on February 20.

1946—Makes Broadway debut in the play *Lysistrata*.

1949—Makes his first film appearance, in a documentary for the U.S. Army Signal Corps.

1950—Has his Hollywood film debut in *No Way Out*.

1958—Becomes first African American to be nominated for an Academy Award for Best Actor for his role in *The Defiant Ones*.

1959—Receives critical acclaim for his role in the Broadway play *A Raisin in the Sun*.

1961—Recreates role of Walter Lee Younger in film version of *A Raisin in the Sun*.

1963—Wins Academy and Golden Globe Best Actor awards for the film *Lilies of the Field*.

1967—Stars in three highly successful films: *To Sir With Love*, *In the Heat of the Night*, and *Guess Who's Coming to Dinner*.

1972—Directs his first film, *Buck and the Preacher*.

1980—Directs hit comedy film *Stir Crazy*.

Timeline

1991—Earns Emmy Award nomination for portrayal of Thurgood Marshall in *Separate But Equal*.

1992—Receives Lifetime Achievement Award from American Film Institute. Receives seventh Golden Globe nomination for *Separate But Equal*.

1997—Earns Emmy Award nomination for playing Nelson Mandela in *Mandela and DeKlerk*.

1999—Receives Lifetime Achievement Award from the Screen Actors Guild.

2001—Receives Honorary Oscar from the Academy of Motion Pictures.

2009—Awarded the Presidential Medal of Freedom for contributions to American culture.

2011—Film Society of Lincoln Center Gala Tribute honors Poitier's life and career .

Morgan Freeman celebrates with his Oscar for Best Supporting Actor for *Million Dollar Baby* at the 77th Academy Awards in 2004.

Morgan Freeman

One film director summed up Morgan Freeman's immense range as an actor by saying:

> When professionals talk range, the names that you hear most often are Robert De Niro, Meryl Streep and Morgan Freeman. It's that indefinable quality that only the greatest actors have to submerge themselves in radically different roles, to make you think in each one of them, "He was born to play that." A lot of actors have that authority in one or two or even three roles, but Morgan has it in everything he does.[1]

Morgan was born in Memphis, Tennessee, on June 1, 1937. His father, Morgan Porterfield Freeman, was a barber, and his mother, Mayme, worked as a nurse's aide and as a teacher. During his childhood, Morgan lived with various relatives in Chicago and Mississippi. His parents quarreled often before they finally separated.

When Morgan was around twelve, his family settled in Greenwood, Mississippi. While living there, Morgan developed his longtime interests in the movies and acting. He scavenged bottles for deposit money to buy movie tickets and study the actors on the screen.

"I went to the movies every day," Freeman recalled. "My idols were Gary Cooper [and] Spencer Tracy. Of course by the time that I graduated from high school, there was Sidney Poitier, picking all the roles that I wanted."[2]

After being encouraged by some of his teachers, Morgan began acting in school plays.

While in the seventh grade, he got a part in a one-act play that won both a district and a state championship. Morgan received an award for being the best actor in the competition.

After graduating from high school, Morgan was offered a partial scholarship to study theater at Jackson State College in Jackson, Mississippi. He turned it down and opted instead to enlist in the Air Force. He had decided that he wanted to become a jet pilot.

Morgan got high scores on his Air Force placement tests. Yet, they assigned him to duty as a radar mechanic. That was a tremendous disappointment that Freeman attributes to racism. "The Air Force was not ready then to encourage a black fighter pilot," Freeman told an interviewer.[3]

Following his Air Force discharge in 1959, Freeman moved to California to look for acting jobs in Hollywood. After a couple of months of fruitless searching, he got a clerical job at Los Angeles City College. The job enabled him to expand his acting knowledge and skills by taking classes there in diction, acting, and voice development.

For a time, Freeman looked for work in both New York and Hollywood. Finally, he found work with a San Francisco musical theater troupe called the Opera Ring. His first appearance with the troupe was in the role of a street singer in *The Threepenny Opera*. It earned him a favorable review, but he left the troupe after having a disagreement about how to play a character in their next production.

Freeman returned to New York and found occasional work as an actor and a singer. In 1964, he made his movie debut as an extra in *The Pawnbroker*. He also found work as a dancer at the 1964 New York World's Fair. In between acting and dancing jobs, Freeman eked out a living by working at a car wash, at the post office, and by selling magazine advertising.

By 1966, Freeman realized that his acting career was getting sidetracked by his work as a dancer.

Clint Eastwood and Morgan Freeman in a scene from *Million Dollar Baby*

He was working as an understudy and chorus member of a touring show called *The Royal Hunt of the Sun* when one of the lead actors collapsed onstage. That was when Freeman finally got the opportunity to act instead of dance.

"After that, my acting career just took off," Freeman would later recall.[4]

Roles followed in both Broadway and regional theater productions. But it was a recurring role in a children's television show that gave him steady employment and financial stability for the next few years. In 1971, Freeman began playing a disc jockey named Easy Reader on the PBS show *The Electric Company*.

The show ran for five years, but Freeman got tired of playing the role. He started drinking heavily and developed ulcers. Freeman was also having marital problems, and he divorced his first wife in 1979.

Returning to stage revived Freeman's acting career. He started getting good roles that earned him critical acclaim and prestigious awards. In the play *The Mighty Gents* (1978), his portrayal of Zeke, a broken–down alcoholic, earned him a Drama Desk Award and a Tony nomination. Two years later, he won an Obie Award for his performances in two plays, *Mother Courage and Her Children* and a production of Shakespeare's *Coriolanus*.

Freeman's success as a stage actor attracted the attention of movie producers. His role as Fast Black, a ruthless and sadistic pimp in the film *Street Smart* (1987), won him the first of four Academy Award nominations. Three years later, he was nominated again for recreating an Obie Award–winning role he had played onstage— Hoke Colburn, a modest, down to earth chauffeur—in *Driving Miss Daisy*. Once again, he was denied an Academy

Award, but the role won him a Golden Globe Award for Best Actor in a Comedy or Musical.

His third Academy Award nomination came for playing prison inmate "Red" Redding in *The Shawshank Redemption*. Freeman's restrained performance as the veteran convict who befriends the falsely convicted Tim Robbins also won him nominations for the Golden Globe and Screen Actors Guild Awards.

In 2004, Freeman gave the performance that earned him the Academy Award that had eluded him for so many years. In *Million Dollar Baby* he played an aging ex-boxer, Eddie "Scrap Iron" Dupris, who mentors a determined woman boxer played by Hilary Swank. Critic Roger Ebert called the film "a masterpiece, pure and simple, deep and true."[5] While taking note of Freeman's fine acting, Ebert also praised his work in narrating the film: "The voice is flat and factual: You never hear Scrap going for an affect or putting a spin on his words. He just wants to tell us what happened."[6]

Well into his seventies, Freeman has won practically every major screen and stage acting award. But no matter how many awards he wins, Freeman still firmly believes that acting is more important than stardom. He continues to look for roles where he can play interesting and memorable characters.

"I like character roles," Freeman acknowledges. "Somewhere back there I really came to the conclusion in my mind that the difference between acting and stardom was major. And that if you become a star, people are going to go to see you. If you remain an actor, they're going to go and see the story that you're in."[7]

Morgan Freeman Timeline

1937—Born on June 1 in Memphis, Tennessee.

1950—Wins his first acting award in Mississippi school competition.

1955—Graduates from high school in Greenwood, Mississippi. Turns down a partial scholarship to Jackson State College in Jackson, Mississippi, to enlist in the Air Force.

1959—Discharged from the Air Force; begins to pursue an acting career.

1962—Joins the Opera Ring, a San Francisco–based troupe.

1964—Makes his first movie appearance, as an extra in *The Pawnbroker*.

1967—Marries Jeanette Adair Bradshaw.

1971–1976—Regularly appears as Easy Reader on the PBS show *The Electric Company*.

1979—Divorces Jeanette Adair Bradshaw.

1980—Wins an Obie Award for performances in the plays *Mother Courage and Her Children* and *Coriolanus*.

Timeline

1983—Marries costume designer Myrna Colley-Lee. Wins second Obie Award for his role in *The Gospel at Colonus*.

1987—Gets Academy Award and Golden Globe nominations for his role in *Street Smart*.

1988—Wins a third Obie for role in the stage production of *Driving Miss Daisy*.

1989—Gets second Academy Award nomination and a Golden Globe Award for role in the film version of *Driving Miss Daisy*.

1994—Role in *The Shawshank Redemption* earns him nominations for Academy, Golden Globe, and Screen Actors Guild awards.

2004—Wins Golden Globe Award and Best Supporting Actor Academy Award for *Million Dollar Baby*.

2009— Appears in *Invictus* in role of Nelson Mandela, first black president of South Africa.

2011— Honored with the American Film Institute's 39th Lifetime Achievement Award on June 9.

2012—Received the Cecil B. DeMille award at the Golden Globes award ceremony.

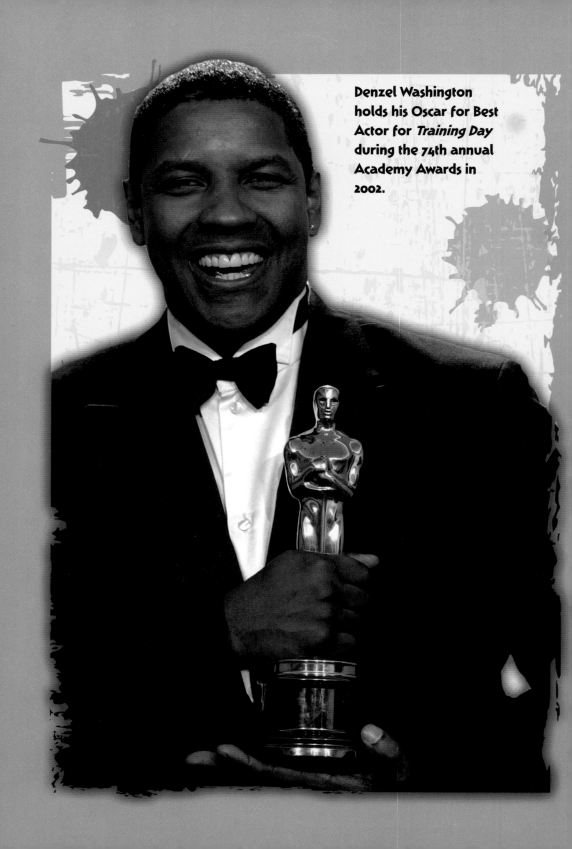

Denzel Washington holds his Oscar for Best Actor for *Training Day* during the 74th annual Academy Awards in 2002.

Denzel Washington

Denzel Washington has become one of the most honored African–American actors by seeking out and playing parts in films like *Philadelphia* and *The Pelican Brief* that weren't specifically written for an African–American actor. In the process, he's won two Academy Awards and two Golden Globe Awards, and has become an international star.

Denzel was born in Mount Vernon, New York, on December 28, 1954. His father, also named Denzel, was a Pentecostal minister, and his mother, Lennis, was a beautician. Denzel, the second of three children, grew up a strict household where drinking, smoking, and swearing were not allowed. He didn't see many movies as a child because his father only allowed his children to watch biblical movies and Disney animated features.

Denzel was a polite and obedient child until his parents divorced when he was fourteen.

Their divorce shattered his world and turned him into an angry and rebellious teenager. He angrily rejected his father's religion and his parents' values. "I rebelled and got angry and started beating people up at school," Washington recalled. "I rejected everything."[1]

Denzel's mother hoped that his attitude and behavior could be changed by sending him off to a boarding school. She enrolled him at Oakland Academy in New Windsor, New York. Denzel excelled at sports there, but was unremarkable as a student. Still, his grades and test scores were good enough for Denzel to be accepted at Fordham University in New York City.

Denzel entered Fordham in 1972 planning to become a physician. He majored in pre-med, but soon changed his major to journalism. And then, during the summer after his sophomore year, he had an experience that caused another change in plans.

Denzel was working at a YMCA summer camp in Connecticut. After he took part in a talent show put on by the camp staffers, some of the other camp counselors praised him for his work and for the ease and poise he showed onstage. When he returned to Fordham in the fall, Denzel starting taking theater classes.

A Fordham instructor and actor named Robinson Stone became Denzel's mentor.

When Denzel played the title role in the school's production of Shakespeare's *Othello*, Stone got other actors and agents to see Denzel's performance.

"He was easily the best Othello that I had ever seen and I had seen [Paul] Robeson play it," Stone told reporter Hilary deVries. "He played Othello with so much majesty and beauty but also rage and hate that I dragged agents to come and see it."[2]

When he was a senior at Fordham, Denzel landed his first professional acting job in the made-for-television movie *Wilma* (1977). It was a biographical film about

Wilma Rudolph, who overcame physical handicaps to win three gold medals at the 1960 Summer Olympics.

Washington graduated from Fordham with a double major in drama and journalism. He continued his acting studies by earning admission to the American Conservatory Theater in San Francisco. He left there after completing one year of the three-year program. He moved to Los Angeles and then to New York in search of acting jobs.

Washington found work with some African-American theater companies, but it was neither steady nor lucrative. He turned down roles that he found offensive. In 1981 he made his movie debut in the forgettable comedy *Carbon Copy*. Author-critic Les Krantz called the film "a labored, predictable comedy"[3] but added that "Washington is still impressive in a thankless role."[4]

After making *Carbon Copy*, Washington was nearly ready to give up on his dream of being a professional actor. The film was a box-office flop, and he wasn't getting any job offers. He accepted a job at a recreation center teaching children sports and acting. One week before he was supposed to start work there, he landed an important acting role.

Washington was chosen to play the Black Muslim leader Malcolm X in the play *When the Chickens Come Home to Roost*. He prepared for the role by avidly reading Malcolm X's books and listening to tapes of his speeches. Washington also dyed his hair red so he would look more like Malcolm X.

The play closed after only twelve performances, but Washington wasn't unemployed for long. His next stage role was in *A Soldier's Play*, where he played a hotheaded army private. In a review in the *New York Times*, Frank Rich singled out Washington's performance by writing:

Denzel Washington in *Malcolm X* in 1992

"Denzel Washington, who recently scored as Malcolm X in *When the Chickens Come Home to Roost*, is equally effective here as another, cooler kind of young renegade."[5]

While Washington's career as a stage actor was taking off, television producer Bruce Paltrow saw him in *Carbon Copy*. He offered Washington a role in a new hospital drama series called *St. Elsewhere*. Washington had turned down other television offers, but the show offered a decent salary and steady employment. He took the job expecting that the show would be canceled after a few weeks.

"I was tired of breaking my behind for no money," Washington told Diane K. Shah in *Gentlemen's Quarterly*. "I went to L.A. thinking, 'This is only going to be for thirteen weeks...'"[6]

St. Elsewhere ran from 1982 to 1988. The show won twelve Emmy Awards, but it never drew a large audience. Washington's role as Dr. Phillip Chandler was small enough to give him time to take on other acting assignments. In 1984, he recreated the role of private Melvin Peterson in a film version of *A Soldier's Play* entitled *A Soldier's Story*.

The 1987 film *Cry Freedom* earned Washington Academy Award and Golden Globe nominations. He played South African freedom fighter Steve Biko. The film itself wasn't highly praised, but most critics agreed that Washington gave a standout performance.

Two years later, Washington won his first Academy Award for playing Trip, an embittered, illiterate ex-slave turned Union soldier in the Civil War drama *Glory*. The film focused on the heroics of the Union Army's first all African-American unit. Washington prepared for the role by reading all about the Civil War and the harsh, inhumane treatment of slaves in America.

"It was difficult to break myself down and become a primitive man," Washington said, "that was the challenge of this part."[7]

Spike Lee's 1992 film *Malcolm X* let Washington recreate a role he had played onstage, and it earned him an Academy Award nomination for Best Actor. Although he didn't win the Oscar, he did get the NAACP's Image Award for Best Actor. Writer and film critic Robin Wood noted how well Washington portrayed Malcolm X's development from angry ex-convict to committed activist for social change: "Washington convincingly shows us Malcolm's growth from irresponsibility to complete emotional and political maturity."[8]

During the 1990s, Washington became a major star with roles in several well-received and high-grossing movies including *Philadelphia*, *Crimson Tide*, *The Pelican Brief*, and *Remember the Titans* (released in 2000). His stirring portrayal of wrongly convicted boxer Rubin "Hurricane" Carter in *The Hurricane* (1999) earned him yet another Academy Award nomination and a second Golden Globe Best Actor Award.

Washington's performance in *Training Day* (2001) won him a second Academy Award. More recently, his role as drug kingpin Frank Lucas in *American Gangster* (2007) earned him his fifth Academy Award nomination and his third Golden Globe nomination.

In 2007, Washington received praise as both an actor and director for the film *The Great Debaters*. Critic Roger Ebert called it "one of the year's best films."[9] *Washington Times* film critic Christian Toto added, "Washington's ability behind the camera nearly rivals his performance."[10] In spite of such good reviews, *The Great Debaters* did not receive any Academy Award nominations.

The commercial and critical success of *The Great Debaters* indicates that Washington will be directing more movies. "I'm very fortunate to have this new career at this point in my life," he said in an interview with the *Minneapolis Star Tribune*. "It's like I've started over again."[11]

Denzel Washington Timeline

1954—Born in Mount Vernon, New York, on December 28.

1972—Graduates from Oaklyn Academy and enrolls at Fordham University.

1973—Briefly drops out of Fordham.

1974—Returns to Fordham and begins taking classes in the theater department.

1977—Graduates from Fordham and gets first professional acting job in the television movie *Wilma*.

1981—Makes film debut in *Carbon Copy*.

1982— Becomes a regular cast member of the television series *St. Elsewhere*. Wins an Obie Award for role in the play *A Soldier's Play*.

1988—Role as Steve Biko in *Cry Freedom* earns him an Academy Award nomination and a Golden Globe nomination for Best Supporting Actor.

1989—Wins both a Best Supporting Actor Academy Award and a Golden Globe Award for his role in *Glory*.

Timeline

1993—Earns an Academy Award nomination and an NAACP Image Award for playing the title role in *Malcolm X*.

2000—Wins a Golden Globe for role in *The Hurricane*. Role also earns him an Academy Award nomination for Best Actor.

2002—Wins Best Actor Academy Award for *Training Day*.

2008—Earns Golden Globe Best Actor nomination for role in *American Gangster*.

2010—Stars in *The Book of Eli* and *Unstoppable*.

2012—Stars in *Safe House*.

Whoopi Goldberg with her Oscar for Best Supporting Actress for her role in *Ghost*

Chapter 8

Whoopi Goldberg

When Whoopi Goldberg found herself frustrated by the lack of good roles for African-American actors, she created her own roles and her own one-woman show. Doing so has led to an impressive career where she has won practically every major acting and entertaining award.

Goldberg was born Caryn Elaine Johnson in New York City on November 13, 1955, but when she found that her age was a handicap to landing acting jobs, she claimed that she was born in 1949. "I lied about my age for a long time because nobody would hire me to act," she explained in an interview. "Everyone said I was too young. So, when I was twenty, I put six years on my life."[1]

Whoopi grew up in a housing project in Manhattan. Her father, Robert, abandoned his family shortly after Whoopi was born. That left Whoopi's mother, Emma, with the responsibility of raising the infant Whoopi and a six-year-old son, Clyde, all by herself.

Emma worked as a nurse and then as a preschool teacher to support herself and her children. Emma was a strict but loving mother who encouraged her children to follow their dreams. Whoopi began pursuing her dream of being an actor when she was only eight years old. She began appearing in plays at New York's Helena Rubinstein Children's Theater. From then on, Whoopi was determined that acting and performing would be her career.

"That's all I ever wanted to do," Goldberg said.[2]

Although Whoopi loved acting, she didn't like school. Learning didn't come easily, since she had dyslexia, which made reading difficult. She also had difficulty concentrating because she would constantly daydream about a future career as an actor and entertainer. Early in her freshman year, Whoopi dropped out of high school.

For the next few years, Whoopi led an unfocused and undisciplined life. She had two abortions by the time she was fifteen. She experimented with all kinds of drugs before undergoing rehabilitation therapy at Horizon House in New York City. Getting off of drugs proved to be a long and difficult struggle. Whoopi had many relapses before she was able to quit.

"I didn't stop altogether at once," Goldberg admitted. "It took many tries....You fall a lot because it's hard."[3]

In 1973, Goldberg was married for the first time. Her husband, Alvin Martin, had been a counselor at Horizon House. The marriage was brief, but it did produce a daughter, Alexandrea, born in 1973. Goldberg was getting occasional acting jobs, but Alvin worked two jobs to make up for her meager income. Arguments over money and other problems led to a divorce.

"She wanted to be a movie star, and I wanted to pay bills," Martin said.[4]

Goldberg took her infant daughter and moved in with her mother, but they only stayed for about a month. A show business friend of Goldberg's who was driving to California asked if she and her daughter would like to come along. Goldberg quickly accepted her friend's offer. A move to the West Coast would allow her to pursue an acting career, with a possibility of getting into the movies.

For about the next six years, Goldberg lived in San Diego. Acting jobs were hard to find, so she worked a variety of odd jobs—bricklayer's assistant, bank teller, cosmetician in a mortuary. When those jobs didn't last, she collected welfare.

Goldberg found some low-paying acting jobs by becoming a founding member of the San Diego Repertory Theatre and by joining an improvisational group called Spontaneous Combustion. During that time, she changed her name from Caryn Johnson to Whoopi Goldberg.

After meeting a stand-up comic named Don Victor, Goldberg formed a two-person act with him called Victor and Goldberg. He was able to help Goldberg learn comedy, and she helped him learn acting.

"Don is a very good stand-up, and I was this weird actor type, and neither of us could get any work. I wanted to learn what he did, and he wanted to learn what I did."[5]

When Victor failed to show up for a performance in San Francisco, Goldberg was forced to do a solo act. A comedian named David Schein was appearing at the same theatre. He encouraged Goldberg by telling her: "Just do what you do when you work with Don and make the audience your partner."[6]

Goldberg hoped to do twenty minutes of material. But the audience really liked her, so she ended up doing an hour of material. After that, she was confident that she could do a solo act.

Goldberg put together a one-hour show called *The Spook Show*. She played four different characters. The show became popular enough to tour the United States and Europe. Mike Nichols, a veteran Broadway

producer, saw Goldberg give her show in 1983. After her performance, he came backstage and offered to produce her show on Broadway. That was the big break that Goldberg had worked and waited for all those years.

Nichols renamed the show *Whoopi Goldberg*, and Goldberg expanded it to six characters. The revamped show received mostly favorable reviews. The cast album of the show won her a Grammy Award. The show ran for 150 performances before closing in March 1985.

Goldberg's Broadway performance caught the attention of another famous producer. This time it was Steven Spielberg, who had produced hit films such as *Jaws* (1975) and *Raiders of the Lost Ark* (1981). He cast Goldberg in his film *The Color Purple* (1985). She gave a powerful performance in the role of Celie, a young, poor, southern woman who is abused and brutalized by the men in her life.

Her stellar performance as Celie earned Goldberg an Academy Award nomination for Best Actress. She didn't win the Academy Award, but she did get a Golden Globe Award for the role.

She appeared as Guinan, a bartender, on *Star Trek: The Next Generation*, for five seasons beginning in 1988.

In 1991, Goldberg won an Academy Award for Best Supporting Actress in the movie *Ghost*. She played a psychic named Oda Mae Brown who helps Sam Wheat (Patrick Swayze), a deceased businessman, communicate with his grieving widow. Oda's intervention helps to solve the mystery of Sam's murder.

The many favorable reviews Goldberg received included one from Janet Maslin of the *New York Times*, who wrote: "Ms. Goldberg plays the character's amazement, irritation, and great gift for back talk to the hilt. This is one of those rare occasions on which the uncategorizable

Whoopi Goldberg

Ms. Goldberg has found a film role that really suits her and she makes the most of it."[7]

In 2002, Goldberg won yet another major award. Her work as the producer of the Broadway musical *Thoroughly Modern Millie* won her a Tony Award.

Even though Goldberg is one of the few actors who has won five of the most prestigious entertainment awards—an Oscar, an Emmy, a Tony, a Golden Globe, and

Whoopi Goldberg in *The Color Purple* in 1985

a Grammy—she recently claimed that she was no longer being sent scripts. According to her, movie producers were bypassing her in favor of younger and more glamorous actors. In a 2007 appearance on the TV talk show *Larry King Live*, Goldberg announced that she would be retiring from acting to focus on her broadcasting career.

But even if she no longer finds work as a leading lady, Goldberg's versatility as an actor should keep her steadily employed. In the past few years, she has alternated between big-budget movies, documentaries, voice work for animated features, and made-for-TV movies. Most recently she has hosted a nationally syndicated morning radio show and has appeared as cohost of the morning television talk show *The View*.

Whoopi Goldberg Timeline

1955—Caryn Johnson is born in New York City on November 13.

1964—Caryn joins the Hudson Guild, a theater group for young people.

1972—Drops out of high school and seeks treatment for her drug addiction.

1973—Marries Alvin Martin, a drug counselor. Gives birth to her daughter, Alexandrea.

1974—Divorces Martin and moves to San Diego, California, with her daughter.

1976—Becomes a member of the San Diego Repertory Theater.

1979—Joins an improv group called Spontaneous Combustion and adopts stage name of Whoopi Goldberg.

1983—Her one-woman show is seen by Mike Nichols, who offers to produce it on Broadway.

1984—Her show, *Whoopi Goldberg: Direct from Broadway*, opens and runs until 1985.

1985—*Whoopi Goldberg: Direct from Broadway* wins a Grammy Award. Her role in *The Color Purple* wins her an Academy Award nomination for Best Actress.

1988–1992—Appears on *Star Trek: The Next Generation* as Guinan, a bartender.

1991—Her role in *Ghost* wins her an Academy Award for Best Supporting Actress.

1994—Becomes the first woman and the first African American to host the Academy Awards. Her hosting performance gets her an Emmy Award nomination.

1998–2004—Appears as a regular on TV's *Hollywood Squares*.

2002—Wins a Tony Award for producing the Broadway musical *Thoroughly Modern Millie*.

2006—Signs a deal with Clear Channel Radio to host a nationally syndicated morning show.

2007—Announces on *Larry King Live* that she is retiring from acting and will focus on her broadcasting career.

2007–2012—Becomes cohost of popular TV talk show *The View*.

Jamie Foxx

Jamie Foxx started out in show business by doing stand-up comedy. As a comedian, he demonstrated a remarkable talent for doing impressions of celebrities and political figures. But when he began doing serious dramatic movie roles, critics and other actors began to marvel at his ability to become another person.

After Foxx won the Best Actor Academy Award for his portrayal of legendary blues singer Ray Charles in the 2004 film *Ray*, his costar Regina King noted: "Most comedians are brilliant men and women…So I was not surprised by his brilliance, but I was floored by his respect for the craft [of acting]. When [we were] shooting Jamie was nowhere in sight. I was working with Ray Charles. Seriously."[1]

Jamie was born Eric Bishop in Terrell, Texas, on December 13, 1967. His father, Darrell Bishop, was a stockbroker. Darrell later changed his name to Shaheed Abdulah after converting to Islam. His mother, Louise Annette Talley, was a homemaker. Jamie's parents separated before his first birthday.

Jamie Foxx kisses his Oscar at the 77th Academy Awards in 2005. He won Best Actor for his work in *Ray*.

Jamie was raised by his mother's adoptive parents, Mark and Estelle Talley. Jamie's grandmother was a strict disciplinarian. She raised him to be a polite and well-behaved child. But because she was so much older than Jamie, he felt that she didn't really understand him.

"There was a generation gap," Foxx said. "She didn't understand me, but she raised me with an iron fist."[2]

Estelle forced Jamie to start taking piano lessons when he was five. He resented it since his friends would be out playing sports or watching television. But the lessons would pay unexpected dividends later in life. When Jamie was thirteen, he became the music and choir director at his Baptist church. That paid him $75 a week, money that his grandmother made him put into a savings account.

In high school, Jamie excelled at both academics and athletics. He was the starting quarterback for Terrell High School's football team. His grades were good enough to earn him a music scholarship to Alliant International University in San Diego, California. There, Jamie studied classical piano and music theory. He was an adequate student, but the pursuit of a career in comedy would keep him from graduating.

One weekend, Jamie and his girlfriend visited a comedy club in Los Angeles. The club was having an open mic night, where club patrons were encouraged to go onstage and perform. Jamie's girlfriend dared him to try. Jamie accepted the challenge and soon had the audience laughing at his impersonations of comedian Bill Cosby, heavyweight boxing champion Mike Tyson, and then-president Ronald Reagan.

The laughter and applause convinced Foxx to seriously consider a career as an entertainer instead of a musician. He dropped out of school in 1990 and moved to Los Angeles. For about six months, he was a shoe salesman

85

by day and an aspiring stand-up comic at night. When Foxx made the rounds at comedy clubs on amateur night, he had to sign his name on a waiting list of potential performers. After a while, he noticed that there were only a few female names on the list. Because of that, someone with a female name was more likely to be called to perform. That persuaded him to change his name from Eric Bishop to Jamie Foxx.

In 1991, Foxx won the Black Bay Area Comedy Competition. That led to an audition for the comedy/variety television show *In Living Color*. Over one hundred actors and comics auditioned for the show. Foxx was picked over all of them and became a regular cast member of the show. He stayed with the show until the Fox Broadcasting Company canceled it in 1994.

While appearing on *In Living Color*, Foxx made other acting appearances. In 1992 and 1993 he made repeated appearances on the sitcom *Roc*. He also made his first film appearance, in the 1992 Robin Williams movie *Toys*. Yet even while he was enjoying steady employment as an actor, Foxx still wanted to perform as a musician.

In 1994, Foxx was able to get a recording contract. Fox/RCA records produced *Peep This*, a CD of rhythm and blues songs he had written. On the CD, Foxx sang and played the piano. The CD was produced on a low budget, and it didn't get much critical acclaim. Still, Foxx's name was powerful enough to help the sales. *Peep This* debuted at number 12 on Billboard's rhythm and blues chart.

Foxx's next television deal had him starring and coproducing his own comedy show for the WB (Warner Brothers) Network. *The Jamie Foxx Show* premiered in the fall of 1996 and ran until 2001. The show had Foxx playing a character very similar to himself: Jamie King, an aspiring entertainer who had moved to Hollywood

The cast of *The Jamie Foxx Show*. Back of the car (l-r): Christopher B. Duncan, Garcelle Beauvais, and Jamie Foxx. Inside the car: Ellia English and Garrett Morris.

from Texas. The main difference between Foxx and his character was that Jamie King had trouble finding work in show business.

While starring in his own television show, Foxx was still able to take on film roles. Some of those early films did not enhance his standing as an actor. One of them was the 1997 film *Booty Call*. The National Association for the Advancement of Colored People (NAACP) and actor-comedian Bill Cosby both strongly criticized the film for its lowbrow humor and strong sexual content.

Foxx responded by saying that the criticisms were valid, but that even in the 1990s there was still a lack of good movie roles for African-American actors.

"[Cosby] had good things to say and I understand where he's coming from," Foxx told an interviewer. "At the same time, you've got to take what you can get to get to where you want to go."[3]

Whatever negative press Foxx got for *Booty Call* was largely forgotten after his performance in the 1999 Oliver Stone football film *Any Given Sunday*. Foxx played Willie Beamen, a self-absorbed, talented but insecure quarterback who becomes a starter after the team's best two quarterbacks are injured.

Movie reviewer Tobias Peterson praised Foxx's performance by writing that he showed "surprising dramatic range."[4]

88

Another sports-themed movie further enhanced Foxx's growing reputation as a skillful dramatic actor. In *Ali* (2001), Foxx played Drew "Bundini" Brown, who served as the corner man for former heavyweight boxing champion Muhammad Ali. Jess Cagle's review in *Time* magazine said that most of the movie's cast was overshadowed by the performances of Will Smith as Ali and John Voight as sportscaster Howard Cossell, but added, "But if you look closely, you will see that the movie's most tragic and comic moments come from Jamie Foxx."[5]

In 2004, Foxx firmly established his reputation as an exceptional actor by receiving two Academy Award nominations. For his role in *Collateral* as Max, a nervous cab driver who is forced to chauffeur hit man Tom Cruise to one of his assignments, Foxx was nominated for Best Supporting Actor.

Critic Roger Ebert wrote: "Foxx's work is a revelation. I've thought of him in terms of comedy...but here he steps into a dramatic lead and is always convincing and involving."[6]

Foxx's second Academy Award nomination that year came for playing the title role in *Ray*. Foxx gave a warts-and-all performance of legendary musician/entertainer Ray Charles. The movie didn't shy away from the less glamorous parts of Charles's life such as his numerous marital infidelities and his battle with drug addiction.

Along with earning him the Academy Award for Best Actor, Foxx's portrayal of Ray Charles won him yet another glowing review from Roger Ebert. Ebert wrote: "Jamie Foxx suggests the complexities of Ray Charles in a great, exuberant performance...Foxx so accurately reflects my own images and memories of Charles that I abandoned thoughts of how much 'like' Charles he was and just accepted him as Charles and got on with the story."[7]

Since winning the Academy Award for *Ray*, Foxx has had some hits and misses in his recent films. *Stealth* (2005) received mostly unfavorable reviews, while the action/adventure films *Miami Vice* (2006) and *The Kingdom* (2007) got mixed reviews. *Dreamgirls* (2006) has been the most successful both in favorable reviews and ticket

sales. His music career has been more consistent; albums *Intuition* (2008) and *Best Night of My Life* (2010) were both top-ten hits that spawned numerous hit singles.

There's a saying that a movie actor is only as good as his last film. Foxx realizes that, and he hopes to move forward by making good decisions about future roles.

"To me it's about just pushing forward," Foxx told an interviewer. "I have to go back out there and keep making great decisions."[8]

Jamie Foxx Timeline

1967—Born on December 13 in Terrell, Texas.

1986—Graduates from Terrell High School and accepts a music scholarship to Alliant International University.

1990—Moves to Los Angeles to pursue a career as a stand-up comedian.

1991–1994—Works as a regular cast member of the television show *In Living Color*.

1992—Makes his movie debut in *Toys*.

1995—Daughter Corrine is born.

1996–2001—Stars in his own television program, *The Jamie Foxx Show*.

1999—Receives notice and good reviews as a dramatic actor in the film *Any Given Sunday*.

2001—Role of Bundini Brown in the film *Ali* earns Foxx further good reviews as a dramatic actor.

2004—Receives two Academy Award nominations, one for Best Supporting Actor in *Collateral* and a second for Best Actor in *Ray*. Wins the award for *Ray*.

2006—Stars in the movies *Dreamgirls* and *Miami Vice*.

2011—Appears in *Horrible Bosses* and *Rio*.

Halle Berry shows off her Oscar after winning for Best Actress for her role in *Monster's Ball* during the 74th annual Academy Awards in 2002.

Chapter 10

Halle Berry

Because she left modeling to pursue a career in acting, Halle Berry has had to work hard to prove that there's more to her than just stunning good looks. To do that, she's had to take on some roles that have portrayed her in an unflattering light. To her credit, she has succeeded. In 2002, she became the first African American to win an Academy Award for Best Actress, for her role in *Monster's Ball*.

Berry was born in Cleveland, Ohio, on August 14, 1966. She was the second of two daughters born to Jerome and Judith Berry. Jerome was an African American, and Judith was white. Judith's parents disowned her after she married Jerome.

Being a racially-mixed couple was a big strain on Judith and Jerome's marriage. Their fragile relationship was also strained by Jerome's drinking and his abusive behavior. He abandoned Judith and his two daughters when Halle was four years old.

In high school Halle was determined to show her classmates that she was as smart and productive as they were. She was a high-achieving student who was also a cheerleader, editor of the school paper, and president of the honor society. But all of her honors and achievements couldn't shield her from racist attitudes.

When Halle was elected prom queen, she was falsely accused of rigging the election by stuffing the ballot box. The charges led to an assistant principal conducting an investigation. He found that Halle had won the election honestly. But she was stung by the charges.

"That's when it really hit me," Berry told an interviewer. "They like me until I'm representing a symbol of beauty in our school."[1]

After graduating from high school in 1986, Berry enrolled at Cuyahoga Community College in Cleveland. At that time, her goal was to go into broadcast journalism. An internship at a local radio station showed Berry that she wasn't really interested in journalism or broadcasting. By that time, Halle had been enjoying some success as a beauty pageant contestant.

Berry had won the title of Miss Teen Ohio 1986. She had also placed second in the Miss USA competition and third in the Miss World contest. Berry moved to Chicago and used some of her beauty contest connections to help her find modeling jobs. At five-foot-six, Berry was considered too short to be a runway model, but she found some work as a lingerie and catalog model.

Berry left Chicago and moved to New York City after she found a talent manager there to represent her. The manager instructed Berry to give up modeling and focus on acting. She auditioned for a role in a proposed television series called *Charlie's Angels '88*. She didn't get the part and the series never aired, but her screen test made a lasting impression on the show's producer, Aaron Spelling.

Halle Berry

Spelling encouraged Berry to pursue her acting career. In 1989, she got her first acting job, as a brainy model in the ABC situation comedy *Living Dolls*. The role gave Berry nationwide exposure, but the show only aired for three months.

Shortly after *Living Dolls* was canceled, Berry landed an important role in Spike Lee's film *Jungle Fever*. It was a breakthrough role for her. She played a crack addict, and prepared for the role by interviewing recovering cocaine addicts and even visiting a crack house.

"When the policeman put the bulletproof vest on me, I should have said, 'OK, this is ridiculous,'" Berry recalled. "Looking back now, I think that I was crazy, but I didn't know anything about drugs, so I really had to go see it."[2]

Other movie parts followed, but Berry probably got the most attention and the widest audience for her role in the 1993 television miniseries *Queen*. Berry played the biracial grandmother of the author, Alex Haley. In the late 1970s a miniseries based on Haley's book *Roots* had become one of the most viewed miniseries in the history of television.

"Being [from] an interracial [background] myself, I felt that if I had lived back then, then some of those things could have happened to me," Berry said. "I knew that I had to play this part."[3]

Berry won her first major acting awards in 1999 for her portrayal of the ill-fated actress Dorothy Dandridge in the HBO made-for-TV movie *Introducing Dorothy Dandridge*. She was also the film's executive producer. Berry's memorable performance won her both a Golden Globe and an Emmy Award for Best Actress. Martha Coolidge, the film's director, recalled that Berry did an incredible job of recreating Dandridge.

95

Halle Berry in *Introducing Dorothy Dandridge* in 1999

Halle Berry

"Halle's a dead ringer [for Dandridge]," Coolidge said. "She also captured her spirit, her talent and her sensitivity."[4]

Even though she had proven herself to be a talented and hardworking actress, Berry still had to overcome a bias against her good looks. Director Marc Forster was reluctant to cast her in his 2002 film *Monster's Ball*. He thought that her image would prevent her from giving a credible performance as the drab wife of a death row inmate.

"I thought that she'd be too [glamorous] but I saw that she'd be willing to deglamorize herself. I also saw incredible sadness in her eyes from her past, I thought that I'd be able to tap into that."[5]

Forster tapped into the full range of Berry's considerable acting talents. Her portrayal of Leticia Musgrove won her the Oscar for Best Actress and gave her some of the best reviews of her career. One of the most glowing reviews came from critic Robin Clifford, who wrote: "The best thing about *Monster's Ball* is the outstanding performance by Halle Berry....There is a raw power to Berry's performance that outshines everything else in the film."[6]

As with other actors, not all of Berry's films have been critical and financial successes.

Gothika (2003) and *Catwoman* (2004) were both largely panned by film critics and failed to attract large audiences. The latter film won her a Razzie Award for Worst Actress. Berry demonstrated that she had a sense of humor by showing up to accept the award. It was the first time that a movie star of her stature accepted what other actors considered to be a demeaning and mocking award.

In 2006, Berry received a Golden Globe nomination for her role in Oprah Winfrey's made-for-TV movie production of *Their Eyes Were Watching God*. It was the third time that she had been nominated for that coveted award. Most recently, Berry has been involved in the production of two film projects, *Class Act* and *Tulia*. Since movie audiences have learned to see beyond Berry's appearance and appreciate her talent, she should continue to be a major star. For Berry, good looks have always been secondary to acting.

"She knows that acting comes first and looks come second," said John Travolta, who costarred with Berry in *Swordfish* (2001). "Looks are the icing on the cake. The cake is your ability to interpret a character."[7]

Halle Berry Timeline

1966—Born in Cleveland, Ohio, on August 14.

1972—Father, Jerome, abandons Halle, her mother, Judith, and her sister, Heidi.

1986—Graduates from Bedford High School. Wins the Miss Teen Ohio beauty pageant and enrolls at Cuyahoga Community College.

1989—Moves to New York City and wins a part in the television series *Living Dolls*.

1991—Makes film debut in *Jungle Fever*.

1993—Appears in the television miniseries *Queen*. Marries baseball player David Justice.

1996—Divorces David Justice.

1999—Wins a Golden Globe and an Emmy for her title role performance in the HBO movie *Introducing Dorothy Dandridge*.

2000—Involvement in an automobile accident causes her to be fined $13,500 and sentenced to three years of probation and 200 hours of community service.

2000—Appears in *X-Men*; later appears in sequels *X2: X-Men United* (2003) and *X-Men: The Last Stand* (2006).

2001—Marries singer Eric Benet.

2001—Wins Best Actress Oscar for her role in *Monster's Ball*.

2002—Appears in *Die Another Day* as James Bond girl Giacinta "Jinx" Johnson.

2004—Earns $12.5 million starring in *Catwoman*, making her one of the highest-paid actresses.

2006—Receives Golden Globe nomination for her role in *Their Eyes Were Watching God*.

2008—Receives BET Best Actress Award.

2011—Stars in *New Year's Eve*.

Chapter Notes

Introduction

1. Gary White, "Jacksonville Filmmaker Was a Pioneer of 'Race' Movies," The (Lakeland, Fla.) *Ledger*, February 22, 2008, p. D1.
2. Donald Bogle, *Bright Boulevards, Bold Dreams* (New York: One World Books, 2005), p. 365.

Chapter 1
Paul Robeson

1. Martin Bauml Duberman, *Paul Robeson* (New York: Ballantine Books, 1989), p. 11.
2. Ibid., p. 62.
3. Ibid., p. 64.
4. Maxine Block, ed. *Current Biography 1941* (New York: H.W. Wilson Company, 1941), p. 717.
5. Geoffrey C. Ward, "Robeson's Choice," *American Heritage*, April 1989, p. 14.
6. Duberman, p. 260.
7. *The New York Times Theater Reviews, 1920–1970*, vol. 5, 1942–1951 (New York: The New York Times and Arno Press, 1971), p. 249–250.

Chapter 2
Ossie Davis

1. Ossie Davis and Ruby Dee, *With Ossie & Ruby: In This Life Together* (New York: William Morrow and Company, Inc., 1998), p. 7.
2. Henry Louis Gates Jr. and Evelyn Brooks Higginbotham, *African-American Lives* (New York: Oxford University Press, 2004), p. 215.
3. Samuel L. Leiter, *Encyclopeda of the New York Stage, 1940–1950* (New York: Greenwood Press, 1992) p. 319.

4. Davis and Dee, p. 242.
5. Goodman Theatre, "Goodman Theatre Begins 2005–2006 Season in the Albert with Major Revival of Hit Broadway Musical *Purlie*," August 15, 2005 <www.goodmantheatre.org/news/pressroom/releases/081505PurlieRelease.aspx> (November 8, 2011).
6. *The New York Times Theater Reviews, 1920–1970*, vol. 7, 1960–1966 (New York: The New York Times and Arno Press, 1971), p. 433. Reprint of review by Howard Tauman, September 29, 1961.
7. Davis and Dee, p. 336.

Chapter 3
Dorothy Dandridge

1. Donald Bogle, *Dorothy Dandridge: A Biography* (New York: Amistad Press Inc., 1997), p. 304.
2. Ibid.
3. Ibid., p. 551.
4. Jessie Carney Smith, ed. *Notable Black American Women* (Detroit: Gale Research Inc., 1992), p. 2G48.

Chapter 4
Ruby Dee

1. Charles Moritz, ed. *Current Biography Yearbook 1970* (New York: H.W. Wilson Company), 1970, p. 108.
2. Ibid.
3. Ossie Davis and Ruby Dee, *With Ossie & Ruby: In This Life Together* (New York: William Morrow and Company, Inc. 1998), pp. 91–92.
4. Ibid., p. 153.
5. Frank N. Magill, ed. *Magill's Survey of the Cinema English Language Films*, Vol. 2, Second Series (Salem Press: Engelwood Cliffs, N.J., 1981), p. 693.

6. Moritz, p. 109.
7. Susan King, "Ruby Dee's Big Break," <www
   .theenvelope.latimes.com/columnists/contenderqa/
   env-ruby-dee-gal14jan14,0,2804548.column>
8. Ibid.

Chapter 5
Sidney Poitier

1. Jeremy K. Brown, "Sidney Poitier," *Current
   Biography Yearbook 2000* (New York: H.W. Wilson
   Company, 2000), p. 447.
2. Sidney Poiter, *The Measure of a Man* (New York:
   HarperCollins Publishers Inc., 2000), p. 17.
3. Ibid., p. 57.
4. Bosley Crowtherhoward Thompson, "Screen: A
   Forceful Social Drama; 'The Defiant Ones' Has
   Debut at Victoria," The *New York Times*, September
   25, 1958.
5. Brooks Atkinson, "A Raisin in the Sun," The *New
   York Times*, March 12, 1959, p. 27.
6. Janet St. Clair, "Lilies of the Field," *Magill's Survey of
   the Cinema*, English Language Films, Second Series,
   Volume 3 (Englewood Cliffs, N.J.: Salem Press,
   1981), p. 1376.
7. Ibid.
8. Henry Louis Gates and Evelyn Brooks
   Higginbotham, *African–American Lives* (New York:
   Oxford University Press, 2004), p. 679.

103

Chapter 6
Morgan Freeman

1. Charles Moritz, ed. *Current Biography Yearbook 1991*
   (New York: H.W. Wilson Company, 1991), pp. 229–
   230.

2. Richard Harrington, "Morgan Freeman Meets His Match in 'Lean On Me,' The Actor Finds His Role After A 30-Year Search," *Washington Post*, March 3, 1989.

3. Ibid.

4. Moritz, p. 231.

5. Roger Ebert, "Million Dollar Baby," *Chicago Sun-Times*, January 7, 2005.

6. Ibid.

7. Carol Kopp, "Morgan Freeman Defies Labels," *60 Minutes*, February 11, 2009. <www.cbsnews.com/ stories/2005/12/14/60minutes/main1127684. shtml> (November 8, 2011).

Chapter 7
Denzel Washington

1. Judith Graham, ed. *Current Biography Yearbook 1992* (New York: H.W. Wilson Company, 1992), p. 593.

2. Hillary de Vries, "Low-key Denzel Hits the Heights," *Chicago Tribune*, August 5, 1990.

3. Les Krantz, *Their First Time in Movies* (Woodstock, N.Y.: The Overlook Press, 2001), p. 147.

4. Ibid.

5. Frank Rich, "Stage: Negro Ensemble Presents 'Soldier's Play,'" The *New York Times*, November 27, 1981.

6. Graham, p. 594.

7. Glen Collins, "Denzel Washington Takes a Defiant Break From Clean-Cut Roles," The *New York Times*, December 28, 1989.

8. Robin Wood, "Denzel Washington," *International Dictionary of Films and Filmmakers*, Volume 3 (Detroit: St. James Press, 1997), p. 1254.

9. Roger Ebert, "The Year's Ten Best Films and Other Shenanigans," *Chicago Sun-Times*, December 20, 2007. <RogerEbert.SunTimes.com>

10. Christian Toto, "Denzel Does It All," *Washington Times*, December 28, 2007. From *www .rottentomatoes.com*.

11. "Debaters may give Denzel another win," *St. Petersburg* (Fl.) *Times*, December 25, 2007, p. 2B.

Chapter 8
Whoopi Goldberg

1. James Robert Parish, *Whoopi Goldberg* (Secaucus, N.J.: Birch Lane Press, 1997), p. 19.

2. Charles Moritz, ed. *Current Biography Yearbook 1985* (New York: H.W. Wilson Company, 1985), p. 144.

3. Jessie Carney Smith, *Black Heroes* (Canton, Mich: Visible Ink Press, 1998), p. 266.

4. Parish, p. 43.

5. Ibid., pp. 59-60.

6. Moritz, p. 145.

7. Parish, p. 214.

Chapter 9
Jamie Foxx

1. Ronald Eniclerico, "Jamie Foxx," *Current Biography Yearbook 2005* (New York: H.W. Wilson Company, 2005), p. 179.

2. Carrie Rickey, "Capturing the inner Ray: Jamie Foxx's rendering of Ray Charles is no jerky impressionist's act," *Philadelphia Inquirer*, October 24, 2004, p. H1.

3. Eniclerico, p. 181.

4. Tobias Peterson, "Any Given Sunday," <www .PopMatters.com.>

5. Jess Cagle, "Jamie Foxx: Ali," *Time*, January 21, 2002, p. 126.
6. Roger Ebert, "Collateral" (review). *Chicago Sun-Times*, August 6, 2004. <rogerebert.suntimes .com/apps/pbcs.dll/article?AID=/20040806/ REVIEWS/408060302/1023> (November 8, 2011).
7. Eniclerico, pp. 181–182.
8. Aldore Collier, "Jamie Foxx: The Thrills and Tears of the Ray Charles Story," *Ebony*, November 2004.

Chapter 10
Halle Berry

1. Matthew Creamer, "Halle Berry," *Current Biography Yearbook 1999* (New York: H.W. Wilson Company, 1999), p. 63.
2. Suzanne Ely, "Halle Berry: Her secret source of strength," *Redbook*, March 2003.
3. Creamer, p. 63.
4. Ely.
5. James Robert Parrish, *Halle Berry: Actor* (New York: Ferguson, 2005), p. 81.
6. Robin Clifford, "Halle Berry's performance makes 'Monster's Ball' well worth the effort..." www .rottentomatoes.com.
7. Ely.

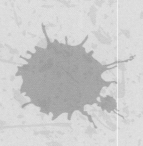

Glossary

corner man—Someone who cares for a boxer between rounds by giving him water and tending to his cuts and swelling.

curtain call—The appearance of a performer or performers at the end of a show in response to applause.

disown—To refuse to accept as one's own.

dyslexia—A disturbance in the ability to read.

extoll—To praise highly.

guffaw—A hearty burst of laughter.

hit man—A paid assassin.

opinionated—Holding stubbornly to one's own opinions.

relapse—To slip or fall back to a former state.

scavenge—To collect by searching.

soothsayer—A person who claims the ability to predict the future.

stature—A level of achievement.

troupe—A company or group of actors.

understudy—An actor who is trained to fill in for another actor who is unable to perform.

valedictorian—A student, usually the one with the highest grades, who delivers the farewell speech at commencement.

Further Reading

Bogle, Donald. *Bright Boulevards, Bold Dreams: The Story of Black Hollywood*. New York: One World Books, 2005.

Epstein, Dwayne. *Denzel Washington*. Detroit: Lucent Books, 2010.

Herringshaw, DeAnn. *Dorothy Dandridge: Singer and Actress*. Edina, Minn.: ABDO Publishing Company, 2011

Lace, William W. *Blacks in Film*. Detroit: Lucent Books, 2008.

Sapet, Kerrily. *Halle Berry: Academy Award–Winning Actress*. Broomall, Pa.: Mason Crest Publishers, 2010.

Slavicek, Louise Chipley. *Paul Robeson: Entertainer and Activist*. New York: Chelsea House, 2011.

Summers, Barbara, ed. *Open the Unusual Door: True Life Stories of Challenge, Adventure, and Success by Black Americans*. Boston: Graphia, 2005.

Todd, Anne M. *Jamie Foxx*. New York: Chelsea House Publishers, 2008.

Internet Addresses

Biography
<http://www.biography.com>

IMDb, The Internet Movie Database
<http://www.imdb.com>

Rotten Tomatoes
<http://www.rottentomatoes.com>

Index

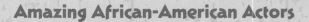